A Purposeful Journey Continues

The Butterfly Experience

Courtney S. Johnson

Published by One2Mpower Publishing
Editor Shawn Jackson
Cover Design by Design Place

Dedication

This book is dedicated to my beautiful daughters Niyla, Hailee, and Cristen. I want you to remember this one thing, no matter what you experience in life, no matter the processes you face, you are beautiful, inside and out. Just spread your wings and fly!

Contents

Introduction

Being able to discover your true identity can be challenging, especially if you are unsure as to who you really are. In my previous book, *A Purposeful Journey: The Process of Enduring While Moving Towards A Meaningful Purpose,* I spoke deeply on my process of enduring struggles, discovering my purpose, the trials I faced, those who supported me, and the transformation of it all. If you haven't read it yet, STOP! Go read that one first because this book is just a continuation of where the journey left off.

The Butterfly Experience is just that. It is an experience of walking into my new beginnings, unafraid of what may present itself ahead of me. It's a process that I welcome, packed with its own challenges. It speaks to the person I have grown to accept, what I have learned, love lost, and love gained. It takes you behind the veil of how I am moving forward. Life is a journey, and I am ready to birth my true self in this next season—welcome to the butterfly experience!

1

The Birthing Process

We all experienced some type of birthing. Whether it was the birthing of your child, sibling, niece, nephew, or even a pet. You have in some way seen the process that one must go through in order to bring something new into the world. As you all may know by now, I am a mother of three. At one point in my life, I could have been a mother of four, but that birth was cut prematurely. See, when I was told that's what I was expecting, I had so many emotions take place. I was scared, nervous, and excited all at the same time. To be honest, I really did not know what to expect because it was something new. To make matters worse, I later found out I was indeed pregnant, but there was nothing inside of me. *Wait! So, you're telling me I am gaining weight for nothing?* This was the question I asked my doctor once they gave me the news. My body was literally proceeding as if I was still carrying my baby, but the embryo sac was completely empty. Apparently, the fetus did not develop, and my body did not get the message.

Long story short, that excitement I was beginning to feel quickly turned into pain as I faced a life-or-death situation. I went from excited to give life to asking the Lord just to preserve mine. It was a very scary moment, one that I often think about. It was my first-time experiencing surgery and giving birth unofficially. It wasn't until this past year that God allowed me to think about this birthing process. I was having a thought of how someone could be pregnant with nothing, and God quickened my thoughts. He simply told me, "You were not pregnant with nothing; I impregnated you with purpose." For those of you that may have been too deep, but what I took from that was even though the embryo sac was empty, God placed his purpose inside of me. I am the one that will give birth to many. Still too deep? Okay, I'll break it down even more. In the natural, all I could see was an empty embryo sac; but in the spiritual, God gave me my assignment as to what he was calling me to fulfill in the earth even though I could not process at that moment how I could not be pregnant with a physical baby. I believe God was using that moment to plant something in me. Y'all, I was pregnant with purpose!

Pregnant with Purpose

When I thought it was meant for me to give physical birth to a baby boy or girl, at that moment, it really wasn't. Indeed, about six to seven months later, I gave birth to a healthy baby girl that's now twelve years old. But God filled me with a purpose back then. Again, I only received this revelation a few months ago, and it has been blowing my mind ever since.

Once you understand the scripture, and I am paraphrasing, God uses everything for your good. What could have been perceived as a horrible situation, God used that memory as a point of revelation. God simply revealed to me that he planted his dreams, goals, and desires for my life inside of me so that one day I would give birth to that purpose. Some of us have been pregnant with purpose for a very long time. We have been experiencing all kinds of pain, thinking it's something natural. Well, honey, I am here to tell you the weight you are carrying was purpose. Yes, you are experiencing the weight of carrying your overdue purpose. Trust me, you are not in this process alone. It was months, maybe even years, before I truly understood this myself. But now that I am aware of my cycle, I know when God is trying to get me to birth something.

It's like any other pregnancy. You go through the motions, but instead of a physical birth, it is a spiritual birthing. I can only speak for myself when I tell you this. It is not something that you should be able to take lightly. It will cause you to stretch beyond measures. It will make you nervous and nauseous. You will develop pains all over, along with fluctuating emotions. I am telling you, when God is trying to get you to bring forth something new, it will be like you are about to give birth to a newborn baby. The real question is, are you ready to push?

Labor and Delivery

Now you have taken the test and realized you are officially pregnant. You have cried and prayed, and God has confirmed that indeed you will give birth to your purpose. Now you must be thinking what else could possibly be next? Well, you guessed it; preparing for labor and delivery. The hardest part really is just accepting the fact that God is trying to do something new through you. I say it's hard because most of the time, we question why or how you will be able to carry out something as amazing as fulfilling a purpose. When God told me I would give birth to many, I can honestly say I ran from the thought of being used in such a way. When after sitting in my quiet place and really consulting with him, God explained to me I would not be in this process alone. He told me all I had to do was trust him. God simply stated I would not have to go through labor and delivery alone. Don't you realize, for those who truly believe, we serve an awesome God that would not allow us to experience any process alone. This understanding only comes with a true relationship with him.

Once I knew I wasn't going to be alone, and God was going to be right there coaching me through it all, the joy in giving birth fell upon me. I began to get excited. I felt the need to celebrate such a joyous occasion until I was yet again stopped dead in my tracks. God said, "You cannot have any and everybody in the labor room." That right there blew my mind yet again. I can recall when I gave birth to all three of my daughters, I had to have a C-section where the doctor has to do surgery to extract the baby from the womb. In the operating room, I had to make the decision on who was going to be there by my side during the process. It was a hard decision, but I decided the father of my daughters should be there in order to see the birth of their seed.

In this case, God gave me the same exact choice but told me to be wise, for not everyone deserves the privilege of seeing purpose manifested up close. See, we get so caught in the excitement and want everyone to be there. God is excited too, but you should understand that moments such as these are not meant for public sharing. They are to be considered intimate and sacred. Therefore, I advise you to be wise in deciding who you would allow in that intimate space with you. Make sure the individual shares in the same birthing plan as you do. You want to make sure they are also in alignment with God and the mission of the delivery. In this space, you do not need individuals that are going to sit around and spectate, but those that are willing to step in as midwives to help coach you through the process. You need those people that are willing to tell you it's time to push. Push, baby, push!

Push, Baby, Push!

When it gets closer to your due date, you get that urge to push. As for me, when I gave birth to my daughters, like I mentioned, I had to deliver via C-section. Was that something I wanted? No! It was something that had to happen in order to deliver the baby safely. See, I went into the hospital two days after my expected due date. *Yes, I had a very stubborn child, still is to this day.* They tried everything to get me to dilate, but it was not working. I was told because I had a pelvic kidney, my uterus was not able to contract on one side of my body. I asked the question, "How could that happen?" The doctor simply stated it could have developed when I was being conceived in my mother's womb. The end result was I probably would never deliver my babies through natural childbirth. Therefore, I never experienced the process of having to push naturally.

Whereas in the spiritual side of things, God allowed me to experience the pressure of having to push, and man is it heavy. I mean, that pressure weighed down on me so heavily I just knew it was going to take me out, but I was not alone. God positioned me around individuals that could see my birthing. They coached and prepared me for what to expect. They were the only ones allowed in my birthing room. When you are in a process, God will send individuals that are assigned to your purpose. He strategically placed them there just to make sure you do not miscarry or deliver too soon or too late. This tribe was amazing! They gave me comfort in knowing everything would be alright and that what I was carrying would shift the world. Oh, and when I felt like I couldn't push, they were right there saying, push, baby, push. I just knew that it was time. I could not delay this birthing any longer. No matter how afraid I was, or unprepared I thought I was, I knew it was something that could no longer be delayed. God needed this transformation to take place. I sucked it up, gave God my yes, and prepared to birth everything God placed on the inside of me.

Before I could really birth, there were some things I needed to make sure were in place. You know, just like you have to make sure the baby bag is packed, and your aftercare bag is all packed beside the door. Well, God simply stated I had to go into this birthing completely empty. He stated all I needed at that moment was him; no bags were required. Therefore, any baggage that I may have had from previous seasons of my life had to be cleared. I couldn't take past hurts, failures, or loss with me, for what I was being birthed into required that I was open and ready to receive.

Your purpose is going to shift you into new levels, which will require you to come with nothing. You will have to recognize when it's time to push and push pass everything you will feel. Will it be easy? Goodness, no! But, it will be worth it. Transformation is a process that will allow new births to take form. If you have never experienced one, you will soon as you decide you are ready. See, I had to make up in my mind that no matter what, I will say yes to purpose. But that comes with being okay with releasing what was, in order to accept what is new. You cannot move forward in your purpose, holding on to what you use to have. It will take releasing past relationships, old ways of living, people, places, and things. Sometimes it will mean moving to a new city or state with nothing. The true question you must ask yourself, "Are you willing, ready, and able to move forward with your transformation?"

2

Moving Forward

Now you are here in this new state of mind, not fully understanding what's next. You have just given birth to your purpose. Maybe it was a book, a new assignment, a business, or whatever. The point is, it's a new beginning. Last year after writing book one, I was in that same exact place of new beginnings. I did not know what to expect. I knew what I was supposed to do, but the question of how to move forward stuck with me. Those individuals that were once there had moved on to their next assignment. I felt like I was back to where I first started in this initial process of submitting and saying yes. The only difference was I knew I had a better relationship with God and knew that this was where I wanted me to be. I had to yet again humble myself and seek God for the answers. I had to know that I would not be able to move forward in any process without first asking him for his provisions and plans.

God does not want us to feel like he has left us to figure out how to move on our own. Yet, I believe in these moments, he is simply showing us how to diligently and intentionally seek him for the answers. After launching my first book, it was only God that recommended I take the book on a six-city book tour. I give him all the credit because I had no thoughts of doing such a thing. So, when I was met with the idea, I sought after him to determine what cities and what dates I would be heading to. I often got the question of could I change this or that when it came to those plans, and I would simply say, "Not without consulting my agent." See, God was my manager. He was the one that set the calendar, and all I did was follow the plan. So before I could change or moved anything, I had to make sure it was in alignment with the purpose.

Too many times, we jump out there on our journeys without any guidance of structure, thinking we know it all and find ourselves out of alignment with our purpose. I tell my girls all the time, make sure whatever you do, you are doing it with God's intentions. I mean, what sense does it make to do something, and it does not hold any value towards your purpose? Therefore, in this part of your process, you want to be very intentional about the paths you take.

Look Straight Ahead

When God sets you out on this new journey, it's one that will require you to keep your eyes looking forward. Now you may say, "Well, is it okay for me to reflect?" Yes, but remember you are made new in this transformation, so what are you really reflecting on? In this case, if you are reflecting on the birthing process, then maybe yes, that's something to take into consideration, but that's it.

You don't want to get caught up thinking about your past too much because it will more than likely cause you to take an unexpected U-turn, thinking you may have missed something. The goal and objective of your transformation is to renew yourself daily so that you can continue to move forward in your purpose. Trust me. I know how it feels to want to revisit certain things from my pasts, but I have to remind myself that I am elevating higher; those things were part of my previous stage. Never have you seen a butterfly go back to doing those things that it once did when it was a caterpillar, do you? So why would you want to spend precious time going back to something you once was? My advice to you is to keep your eyes forward and don't look back.

19

What concerns you now is far more important than those other things. I think of it as the "outer cocoon phase." You now have taken on your new form, and things are looking very brand new. You are looking and examining how much you have grown, changed, and developed; you may not even recognize yourself. But that's okay! You are stepping into your greatness, your transformation. It's now time to see what life is like from a new perspective.

3

Beautiful Wings Unfolded

Not every process is one that starts off picture-perfect. Honestly, I don't think any process is ever perfect in the beginning stages, but we move forward. When it came to entering into this new season of my life, I had to get the understanding under my belt, not everything will go as I would want them to be. That life is a marathon and not a race. See, we try so hard to make things beautiful from start to finish and miss the process inbetween. We want to skip by the ugly parts, dismiss the pain, and jump straight to the glory of it all. God does not intend for us to go through anything quick. We must be willing to peel back each layer, one by one.

Like I mentioned in my first book, I thought I had life all figured out. I knew who I wanted to marry, how many kids I wanted, what type of career I would be working, and it was perfect—until I met my maker. You heard me; God stopped me and corrected me and said he had great things in store. I am sure I am not the only one that has experienced this, and I can bet you that I will not be the last one. But what I can assure you is I am now free of thinking things are perfect.

We must get to that place of just being able to endure what it is that we go through. Life, in a nutshell, is an entire process that has the ability to become beautiful over time. The true question is, are you willing to wait through that process to watch your wings develop? When I was given the mantle of birthing, I gave myself false beliefs that it would be this perfect thing that I would do, dismissing the fact that rising to the occasion, nothing has been perfect. I then felt defeated because I allowed myself to believe that lie. We must get out of telling ourselves things that will only boost our emotions and start holding ourselves more accountable. Every process will be different, and you will indeed go through stuff, but you must be willing to endure those things in order to see the fruits of what it could produce.

My transformation season has been one that I have welcomed willingly because I understood what I meant to really be free in mind, body, and spirit. I knew just from all the trials that it was going to push me to become greater, and my bloodline was dependent on that growth. As many of you, myself included, we have people that are watching our development. They are taking notes. They are waiting to see if we break under pressure. You know the saying, "Diamonds are created under pressure?" Well, you must consider yourself to be that diamond. I, on the other hand, consider myself to be that butterfly.

Once a butterfly is out of its shell, it no longer thinks as a caterpillar, for that identity has died. It is now a new thing ready to take on the world. It has now discovered that it has wings, and they are meant to soar beyond its prior limitations. What once burden me no longer has that control over me because I now have discovered I have the ability to fly above it all.

If you ever noticed or studied a butterfly, you will see that they come in many different shapes, sizes, and colors. Their wings are designed in such a way that gives them their own identity. I believe I am created in such a special way that you will not find any other person like me on this earth. I have reached a place in my life where I have become one with my abilities to use my gifts to fly high, exceeding those limiting beliefs that once kept me grounded.

Again, when you first start out on your journey, you will not come in knowing how to do everything in order to become successful. You will have to get comfortable with being uncomfortable. And if you are a butterfly like myself, you know that you will not be able to fly from the start. You must first become one with the fact of having something new that will take you to those higher levels. You must be willing to see the beauty of allowing your wings to develop. If you try to fly too soon, you risk the chances of damaging that which is supposed to take you to your greater. Don't rush thinking you are missing out on something. Enjoy the beauty of the unfolding of your wings. Embrace the fact that you are created in a newness many will take pleasure in seeing. Once your wings are fully developed, you are ready to take flight. God will give you the push that it's time, but until then, just enjoy the process of being developed. Trust me when I say this, your newness will open up doors to new levels creating new opportunities.

4

New Levels, New Opportunities

In this new season of transformation, I have discovered that so many new doors have been placed right before me. Some I kind of saw coming, but a great many of them I had no idea could take place at this level. That's the greatness of being connected to a higher source. Knowing whose you are and who you are holds much weight when walking through a process. My journey would not be what it is today without me stepping fully committed to my transformation.

Being unable to accept everything that I had to go through would have anyone asking, "Is this really happening?" There were plenty of nights I sat in my car, yes in my car, because I allow that space to be alone to think and hear from God. I heard God say, "It's going to continue to happen as long as you trust in your process." WOW! So what God was telling me was all I had to do was believe in my process and the ability to use what I already had in order to get to this place? God simply stated, "Yes!" Sometimes we do not get to our new levels, not because of anything someone else did not do, but because of our own failure to just believe in our process.

New Levels of Thinking

Transformation required me to alter a few things now versus later. No longer could I put off taking care of some things because they were connected to my next level. If I wanted to shift, there were some things I had to get in play NOW. The biggest thing was I had to adopt a new way of thinking. Transformation is the renewing of your mind. Well, I had to understand it was not something you do one time, and that's it. No, I have to consistently be in a state or renewal. The way I thought about certain places, people, and things had to change. I had to allow myself to think positively daily. I am not saying I was this bubbly person all the time, and nothing ever went wrong. What I am saying is when negative thoughts try to occupy more space than was allowed, I quickly get my mind on things that are good. This is another reason why I truly believe in keeping a gratitude journey. It's where I keep those things that I am grateful for.

Just knowing I have tools at my hands that I can implement has been one of the best things ever for me. Not everyone is in this exact position, I get that, but it is not hard to get to that place. Understand that your next level is attached to how quickly you are able to shift your thinking. The true task is creating that awareness and working towards it every day.

Positioned for Opportunity

Now that you have gotten into a routine that allows you to tap into a greater self, you can best believe you will meet new opportunities at the door. When I started thinking on a higher level, I was introduced to individuals that pushed me to do the unexpected. I knew they were positioned so strategically by God because everything they requested of me was things I have only revealed to God. They were connected to my next level, which led to my next opportunity. I had to be in the proper position in order to receive that which was already waiting for me.

Too many of us are always requesting God to do major things in our lives, but we are out of position. I had to learn a lot of this the hard way. Now that I know better, I am doing better. I am still not where I want or should be, but I am so grateful that in this process, I have grown. I have a clear understanding that when opportunities present themselves, the best thing for me to do is commit first and figure the rest out later. You might think that is risky, and I would agree with you, but what is life without taking risks? We risk our lives every day, any time we decide to step foot outside our homes. What I am suggesting is if you are willing to take a risk, make sure that you are already walking in proper alignment with the will of God. The choices I make are coming out of the late-night prayer, talks, and cries that I had with God.

The opportunities I am experiencing in this part of the journey have been planted in me for some time. The only thing that was really stopping me was me. The only thing stopping you is the limiting belief that things need to be better in order for you to start. I am here to tell you that is a lie. Yes, it can be scary to step outside of your comfort zone, as a new creation, ready to accept new things. It is time to tap in and receive the love that awaits you on the other side of opportunity. I am here to tell you, love is not always something you look for but will oftentimes find you right where you are.

5

Love On Me the Right Way

On my previous journey, you know, before I made my full transition, I believed that I had found love. Yes, I was head over heels in love. I mean, I was receiving love from all ends. I had a man, my kids were loving me, and I felt the love of God all over me. I considered life to be good.

What if I told you that what we sometimes consider great, could actually be taking away from us. Not because of anything that you may have done, but simply because God has something better for you. Now, this is not a tell-all book about anything, but simply one that gives you insight for the journey ahead. You have had your whole entire life planned out, from the husband to the kids, to everything. But if it is not in alignment with what God desires for you, you will not fully experience the love God has for you.

That's what my journey has come to. I was thinking one thing, but God was showing me a completely different view. God simply stated that he wants to love me the right way. Man did that blow my mind. See, when God first told me he loved me, it was audible; it was a moment I would never forget. If you ever heard the song, *Why I Love You*, you will definitely understand the type of relationship that me and God have.

God simply just wants to love me, and he will stop anything that will try to take that number one position. I knew that even though things didn't turn out how I wanted them to, God gave me something in that process. He gave me an understanding on how I should be loved in this season. I learned more about myself in this season than I have ever known in my entire being. I was able to identify with His love in human form. If you ever get to this point, you will know that it's a love that will last forever.

Self-Love Is Needed

I honestly thought I would have fallen into a deep depression after my previous relationship simply because it was my norm. I think my belief of God being the orchestra of all things, and only wanting the best for me, is why I was able to see the good in what he was doing in this situation. I allowed God to take me through this process. I gave all my hurt, questions, and concerns to him. In return, God gave me peace, understanding, clarity, and wisdom. I received straightforward instructions on what and how to move forward. I became totally dependent on the voice of God. I began to take more care of myself. I started to love myself all over again. It's one thing to let yourself go when you go through a bad break up. But what about the good ones? I knew that in order for me to continue moving, practicing self-awareness, and self-care, I had to be at the forefront. Now you may say, Courtney, I hear you, but I loved him. Honey, how can you love someone else if you don't love yourself? Let that marinate for a moment.

Some things I started to incorporate into my daily routine was meditation based on clarity and wisdom. See, I knew how I wanted to be moving forward, but I lacked the clarity and understanding on how to do so. Therefore, I meditated daily. I am talking about all day, every day. I trained myself to shift my thoughts. When I felt myself going down that lonely, depressing road, because I am still human, I had to switch up my thinking. At first, I can be honest, that was not the easiest thing to do. It was actually really hard, but I kept practicing it. I refused to let those negative thoughts overcome me. So, I made a decision that when things started to go left, I would go right. And if it was too hard to turn around, I had those accountability partners in place that could help me regain my focus. I can truly say I love my tribe.

Tribal Love

Like I mentioned before, I just love my tribe. They know exactly how to keep me grounded, especially when faced with difficulties and challenges. This past season has really shown me who was for me and who was not. I am not one to share all my problems with others. The majority of the time, I would rather suffer through what I am dealing with versus telling anyone about my sorrows. The greatest thing about having a strong tribe, you never have to tell them what you are going through; they always seem to know the right thing to say at the very moment.

Therefore, when I felt myself questioning what was really going on, my best friend, who I called my sister, confronted me and simply reminded me of the beautiful spirit that I am. She expressed that even though I may have been feeling like I was not loved, she loved me, my children loved me, and eventually, I would find the one that would love me the way God so desired for me to be loved. Just hearing those words provided me with the peace that was needed in order for me to regain focus.

So, ladies, remember, when it comes to love and being in that vulnerable space, you have to believe that God plays a major role in that too. He is the one that knows exactly how we should be loved. Your only true task is to continue to seek after God and his kingdom. Believe that his word is true and that all those things that we really desire have the possibility to manifest. It's time for us to enter into our new phase!

6

Entering a New Phase

When you think about phases, what tends to come to mind is how the moon changes. Imagine with me you are outside your home looking up at the night's sky. If you don't live in the city, you can see all the twinkling stars, and the bright moon. You have made a note of the different shapes and sizes of the moon over the last few nights. Now on this particular night, you are unable to see the moon; therefore, it is in its new moon phase. If you ever paid attention in science, you would know that during this phase, the moon is closer to the sun; therefore, it does not have any shadows. Think about your life and where you are in your current process. You may be experiencing some heat from the sun and not sure of what to do. You are now what I am considering entering your new phase.

In this phase, you are evolving into that new person, taking on a character that has never been seen. You are shifting from what was into what will become. Not all times you will feel comfortable.

Truth be told, if you are transforming, you will never feel comfortable. These different phases will cast a different kind of brightness. You will shine like no other. What others may not have seen in you before, they will now be able to see.

I am in a new phase in my life where I am being exposed to those things that will shift me even more into my greatness. I recognize that those who once saw me can no longer see, and those that couldn't see me are now able to. This phase has elevated my confidence, and I am no longer afraid of the process of shifting. It's something about being able to see yourself in your own process that will motivate you to keep moving. The ultimate goal in this phase is never to stop moving. Before you know it, you will be bigger and brighter in sight to those that were blinded by the lights of the views around them. The key is remembering that it all starts from within yourself.

7

Heightening My Motivation from Within

As a life coach, I hear this all the time, "It's not easy to motivate myself, I need someone to help me." Do you want my honest opinion? You are absolutely wrong! You are the only one that can motivate yourself. Now, is it easy to do? Nope! But it is something one must be willing to work at daily.

I was in this place of believing I had to have all these other things to help motivate me to do what I knew God was calling me to do. From the YouTube videos to the different Facebook lives, I felt I needed all those things to actually push me to get out what was already inside of me. It would be days of just watching and writing and not actually producing before I realized I wasn't being motivated at all. It wasn't until I made the decision that the only way I was going to get anything accomplished was to speak it and do it. That became my motivation.

When you start to see yourself from a third-person point of view, you will understand the only motivation you ever will need is that which is inside of you. I had to look myself in the mirror and declare what it was that I wanted and then go out and do just what I declared. I had to simply give myself a boost or a kick in the tail to really get moving. I had to understand that I couldn't keep looking towards others for the motivation I needed. I just had to believe I had it inside of me all along.

This is where heightening my motivation comes into action. To heighten something is simply to increase the intensity of what's normal. Therefore, I had to get to a place of moving above and beyond what was normal for me. But first, I had to establish a clear understanding of what's my norm. What were those things that I did on a normal basis? Once I answered that question, I was able to establish new goal levels that would push me beyond what I was used to.

See, most people do not like to challenge themselves; therefore, they remain stuck asking the same question, what do I need in order to motivate myself. And again, I say, it's not what do you need, but what are you willing to move beyond. I really had to create higher goals and objectives for myself. Those goals had to be challenging; that way I knew I had to really put in the work to manifest the vision.

8

See the Vision, Become the Vision

It does not take much to become that which you see. If you can envision yourself in a particular place, then you can definitely make it a part of your reality. Last year, as I began this process of transformation, I created a vision of becoming a well-known author. I knew it would not happen overnight, as I was not looking to become an overnight success story. But I knew and believed in my heart that people would begin to know me from my stories. I cannot openly say that I, myself, created the vision, but it was one that God allowed me to have access to. The Holy Spirit simply stated to me if I could see where God was taking me through this process, I could become that which I see.

To me, that was when the real shift started to take place in my mind. I had to really see the vision. Not just a glimpse of it, but really see myself becoming everything God showed me I could be. You know how you create vision boards? Well, it wasn't just any vision board that I created, but one that God had already designed on my behalf. It was so detailed that it literally blew my mind. The visuals that God provided me were timed stamped. I knew that if God wanted me to see it, he must have believed in me so much more than what I could possibly see.

That is the beauty of being in relationship with the Father. You get to have access to the visions, plans, and dreams of God for your life. That's right; God will show you personally everything that he has already mapped out for you. The only thing we must do is follow his commands of becoming that which he has shown us.

Becoming the vision again will not happen overnight. Matter of fact, it can be very overwhelming if you are mentally ready to receive. Once I had an inside view of God's vision for my life, I decided it's up to me to continue on the path that will manifest this vision. Indeed, it challenged me, but I have experienced worse. I knew that this was going to take me to even higher levels. The only person that would stop me from ever achieving any of this would be me. Therefore, I made up in my mind that I had to get out of my own way!

9

Getting Out of My Own Way

Accepting your walk in your new transformed state will require you to move in such a way that will become uncomfortable at times. Nothing about this process that I am on has been comfortable. To be really honest with you, it has been one of the most difficult things I have had to do. I knew the only person that was holding me up from moving forward was me. Yes, I was my biggest hold up in this season.

This revelation has been mind-blowing because when I did decide to move beyond doubt and fear, I would still find myself distracted. Have you ever wanted to do something, but everything else would appear as a priority? That was me and, at times, still me. When it came to realizing in order for me to continue moving in this process, I will have to put some boundaries in place for myself. That means I would have to become more disciplined in my own actions and behaviors. Again, my birthing process will not look like yours, but we will all experience something similar.

Setting up those boundaries is what I believe was the best thing for me. I needed to really position myself to focus on what was in front of me. I really needed to be in the place of preparing for my future. The vision that God has given us will only come into reality if we do our part. As I mentioned in my first book, getting to a place of submission will open up so many doors. It doesn't mean you won't be challenged. What it does mean is that you have agreed to allow God to do the work required through you.

Stepping out of the way in my process has given me two different viewpoints. The first one is what it would be like if I don't move out of the way. And the second one is how it would be if I moved out of the way. If I decided to sit in the way of being comfortable, not doing what's required, and putting no effort towards accomplishing my goals, I would be stuck in transit, meaning I will continue to hold up the blessings that were created for me. On the other hand, if I decide to move my feet, do the necessary steps, and allow God to guide me in every step, I will then reap the benefits and rewards of fulfilling my purpose.

That is all I ever wanted to do was get to a place where I do not have to figure it out on my own. I would rather live each day knowing God is leading and guiding my every move, than me trying to determine if the decisions I am making aligned with my purpose. Everything we do within our process should lead us a little higher in attaining our purpose. Once you have determined what it takes to vibe on a higher level, it becomes your new norm.

10

Learning to Vibrate Higher

We are now at this place where we have this new thing. We just gave birth to purpose, and life began to hit from all sides. You began to have thoughts of defeat, but you bounced back. You started moving forward only to have something else to stop you. You now have determined the only thing that was stopping you was you, and in order to attain purpose, you got to move out of your own way. You may ask, how do you do that? Well, I would suggest learning how to vibrate at a higher level than what you are accustomed to. In order to vibrate higher, you just have a clear understanding of frequency and that you are a spiritual being that travels through this life on frequency waves.

You ever wondered why or how you could simply think about something, and all of a sudden, you begin to see that very thing everywhere you go? Would you believe me if I told you that your thoughts are transmitted through frequency waves and that it allows the universe to align with those thoughts? This is why it is so important to be very mindful of what you think, but also what you speak.

I never really knew all of this before entering into my process. It took for me to study and do plenty of research to attain this knowledge. I knew that there had to be a reason why this was happening, so I took the time to learn.

I became a student of my purpose. If I was going to teach, coach, train, and develop others on how to shift their thoughts, so that it could change their surroundings, I had to understand it for myself. I created a plan that would allow me to think about things. Some things were realistic, and some were just plain right out there. But I centered my thoughts on those things. I took the time to meditate on those things daily. I made sure my posture was one of gratitude and that I was in expectation of those things, removing any doubt.

When I got to the place of truly believing that those things were indeed possible, I felt my life shifted. It wasn't a physical shift, but a supernatural one. I began to see all those things manifested for others very close to me. You know the saying when those around you are starting to get blessed, God is in the neighborhood. I developed the mindset that I was next in line. I began to think more on those things as if I had them in my possession. Not everything was tangible, but they were also qualities that I desired for my life. They were the things I knew I needed to embody in order to fully shift into my higher self.

Higher Self

Discovering my higher being was simply just identifying those things that were greater and positioned me to receive at a higher level. It's only achieved once you begin to live at a higher vibration. But can your higher self exist before you reach those levels? Oh, absolutely! Before I could reach a high level of myself. I would often meditate, seeking guidance from God on how I could tap into my higher being. It is my belief that my higher being resides with him. My higher being is living her fully transformed self, and she is basking in the full favor of God. I believe, every now and then, throughout my process, God allows me to see my life manifested through the eyes of my higher self. It lets me know that the possibilities of achieving everything you desire is closer than we think.

The best way to really get to that place of learning how to shift to higher levels of living again starts in your thoughts. How much time are you really focusing on things that will transform you? Are you seeking that higher level? Are you seeking that higher level, or are you wasting time believing in the negative bad experiences? Are you dwelling on the statement, "Never would I ever?"

11

The Day I Said Never Would I Ever

In reflecting back over any process or challenge we may have, we can always recall a moment where we use the statement, "Oh, I would never do such and such ever again." Only to realize days or months later, you are back doing the very thing you said you would never do. I found myself in that particular situation a few times more than what I would like to recall. But one thing is for sure when you truly believe in your process of transformation those moments become lessons to reflect one.

One moment I would say that I can recall I said I would never, ever do again was refusing to operate out of purpose and obedience. Let me tell you, when you think you won't fall into temptation, it is the very thing you will fall to. I made myself a vow, saying I will always listen to the voice of God; I will never not do what he tells me. You know how we get when we are trying to convince God that we will do what is right. What we fail to remember is that God is the one that has created us. And at that moment, I had forgotten that very thing.

Here it is I am saying all these things, making all these pleads, and God was sitting right there looking at me. God knew that temptation was going to come, and I would fall submissive to it instead of him. And you know what, God was right! When the chance came for me to spend time focusing on something else besides what he had ordered me to do, I left his presence and followed temptation. It looked more appealing, and I made every excuse as to why I made my decision. Even though I vowed to never ever leave God's will, I did.

Now, I don't say all this to make you feel back, but to clearly show you how easy it is for us to step outside of our vows to the Father. What I thought was easier and better only placed me in a position of being disobedient, which in return held up how God was trying to bless me in that season. We must be very mindful of our words to God, keeping in mind he is the God who knows all.

On your journey there will be some things that will look very entertaining, pleasing to the eye, and refreshing. You will have to ask yourself, "Does it fall in line with my purpose?" If we spend all our time chasing after those things that are not in alignment with our purpose, we will lose focus. We will then hold up the next line of blessings that could shift the direction of our bloodline. We have to get out of the mindset that we will never do this and that and acknowledge that if we are not obedient, disciplined, and focused, it could happen. Not everything is outside of our reach. We sometimes have to realize that everything we need in order to achieve our purpose is already on the inside of us. You just gotta use what you got!

12

You Gotta Use What You Got

As a life coach, I have encountered many individuals who believe that there is something that they are missing, and that becomes their reason for why they don't have or believe they are not where they need to be. I want you who are reading this to really understand it is not what you need or believe you are without, but what's within you have yet put to use.

As purposeful beings, we were created with everything we needed in order for us to become successful beings. Over time we have allowed society to cloud our thinking, causing us to believe we need certain titles, education, or material things in order for us to become successful. I have learned it is not what I needed to add to me in order for me to feel I am successful, but it was ultimately my thoughts and the work I did which caused me to think I am becoming successful.

Understanding what you already have within you is a jewel.

It is something not everyone has gained possession of. Some will wander this earth for the rest of their natural life, searching and looking for something external. The power of searching within takes getting to want to know who you are. This journey has taught me that when things are not lining up on the outside, there must be something within me that is out of order. I then take the time to center myself, looking at every part of my being. Once I have found that missing link, I then apply it to where I need things to line up in my life.

I am sure I have some of you that can relate to this, and those of you, I'm pretty sure by the end of this book, you will have gained a sense of clarity. The focus here is to become so in tune with your gifts and those talents you have been blessed to have and begin to put those things to use. It is not always obtaining another degree or taking another training but simply sharpening that which you already have. Simply stated, you just got to get comfortable with using what you got. You gotta get to that place of operating at maximum levels.

Now I am not telling you to work yourself to exhaustion, but to use your gift at its full capacity. My declaration is that before I leave this place called earth and transition to my next phase of life, I want to return to my Father being emptied of all that he has given me. I want those that will hear from me, read about me, or just simply knew my life's story to know that I believed in everything that I possessed, and I understood even though times got hard, I knew I was built for this journey. I knew I could handle everything that was or would have been thrown my way. The key factor was just believing.

13

Know This...I Was Built for This

Going through any process, journey, or just the trials of life, you get to the place of wondering is it all worth it. You may start to develop those thoughts of what's the point. I am here to tell you that when those limiting beliefs start to arise, and trust me, they will, you have to dig deep. You have to pull out that inner fight and believe that you were built for the journey.

There is a song that echoes in my head that asks the question, why not me. Well, many times throughout this whole process, I would ask myself, *why are you going through this? Why are you choosing to deal with some of the things you are going through? Is it really worth it sis?* You guys know the conversations you have with yourself when no one else is around. I would spend most of my day pondering those questions all to hear from God asking, why not me?

God created us to go through all things as long as we knew that it was through his strength that we would make it through. Too often, we spend all of our time trying to figure out why this or that is happening and coming up with a solution, where all God wants us to do is trust him in the process. It is by his strength that we will be able to make it through anything. It is by his strength that our trials and tribulations have not overcome us. So if this is found to be true, why do we still question what it is that we experience or go through?

I truly think, and I am speaking for myself, that the reason why I have fully accepted this is because we are still accepting doubt somewhere. I know when I start to question things more than normal, it is showing me that I am out of alignment, and I have failed to trust my Father in the process. It is not hard to slip away; the true task is recognizing and getting back in order.

In other cases, it is because I give up the fight and just say to hell with it. I know I am not the only one when faced with certain obstacles, you rather just give up than continue to fight. Well, that has been me more than a few times throughout this process. At times, I just feel like there is no need to fight until I get that reminder I am fighting yet again in my own strength. It does not become evident to me until something dramatic happens, and I'm stuck there asking

God, what now? God does not want us to try him after the fact, but consider his ways before it takes flight.

I made the decision no longer can I just quit the fight, but I must make sure I am drawing my strength from my Father. I have learned that being more proactive versus reactive will save me a lot of time, energy, and money. I have discovered no matter what I face, God has created me to be a unique individual with a purpose. I honestly believe he took his precious time to mold, shape, and develop me to be that reflection of him in this earth. You must continue to fight for your purpose every day because at the end of the day, you are the only one that has to live with the results.

At night, once I settle my spirit from all that I have done, I do a self-reflection, taking inventory of all those things I have accomplished for that particular day. I reflect on the conversations I may have had, the people I may have met, or even the actions I may have done. I reflect on those things to see if I fulfilled my mission for that day. Do I get it right all the time? No! But do I allow for grace to take its rightful place in my life? Yes. I understand I am only human, and I will have moments where I will miss my mark. But one thing I try not to do is lose my momentum in achieving that which I am

purposed.

14

Where's Your Momentum Mommy?

My journey has been many different things. It has opened many different doors for me, as well as closed some. Just being able to endure the majority of what I go through has been challenging, but again, it is what I choose to fight for every day. The fight for your purpose hits a little different when you have little ones watching your walk.

Becoming a single parent was not always a part of my ultimate plan. As some of you may have read in book one, I thought I had my whole life planned out until I got pregnant with my oldest. From that point on, I became the mother to two more girls, and they watch everything I do. I always joked around and said, if God wants to slow you down and show you exactly how much of a fool you are acting, he will allow you to get pregnant.

I can openly and honestly say I was that fool. I knew I was doing things I knew I had no business doing. I knew and understood the chances of me conceiving another child was very high, so after finding out about my third child, I made the choice to have my tubes tied. It was a decision that was tough to make because here it is, I was a mom of three and unmarried. People often ask me, what if you get married, and your husband wants kids? My response has always been, if God sent him to me, then he will be aware of my circumstances. It used to bother me a lot to hear those things, but not too much anymore. I have gained peace in knowing that God has given me the opportunity to steward over his creations. Therefore, I could not allow the opinions of those around me to affect my decision.

They Are Always Watching

For those of you who are reading this and you have children, you will relate highly to what I am about to say. You know that no matter what you do and you think no one sees you, there is always someone watching you. I can recall a time I was trying to be sneaky and eat snacks, moving around like a mouse, thinking that if I could just get the chip bag open quietly that my baby wouldn't hear me. The lies, I thought. I mean, as soon as I got the bag open, she was looking right at me. I was like, dang, can I at least enjoy a snack alone?

As my girls got older, I started to notice they would do more and more things like I would, which gave me even more evidence that they were watching me. I became their first example. I was their model on how it was to be done. Therefore, I had to be careful of the things I said, what I did, or how I would act. It was indeed a proven fact that they were watching.

I often tell the story of how I gave birth to all of my girls while going to college; that's why they are so smart. Honestly, I do think that has something to do with it, but my girls had the opportunity to see firsthand the hard work and dedication it takes to achieve your goals. They witnessed the many nights I would stay up late, sometimes not even touching my dinner because I was busy trying to get my papers or assignments done. There have been times where my oldest would ask me if I was okay because she would catch me crying my eyes out due to being tired and stressed from all the work.

My girls have seen the many times I said I was done and I was giving up because I just didn't want to do it anymore. It was in those moments that I gained momentum from their little voices telling me, "Mommy, it's okay. You can do it." It's those moments that I knew I had to continue to fight on. I could not give up because they are watching me.

When you have those little ones that are always on your tail, and you feel like you can't get a break, life becomes hard. I know that if you could just have five minutes to breathe without someone saying, mommy, it would make all the difference. Trust me; I get it. Even with my girls being older, I still feel like I need those moments. But what you must remember is our babies are gifts from God. They are given to us to help assist in their grooming and development so that they too can live a life of purpose.

My girls are now more excited and interested in learning more about what it is that I do. I allow them to witness my life from all perspectives. It brings me much joy just to see how they feel that they too can grow up and become anything that they want. I motivate them, but little do they know, they are the ones that really push me to be the best I can be on a daily basis. I am so blessed to have those girls a part of my journey.

Granted, not every part of my life I am pleased with, and I have apologized to my babies for putting them through some things. But I know we all are on a journey that no man has ever walked on. It is one that was truly created and designed for us. I like to think of it as our very own road less traveled by.

15

Road Less Traveled By

Do you recall the poem, *The Road Less Traveled By*? It was the very first poem that I can recall I had to memorize for an English class in the seventh grade. Just looking at the length of the poem on paper terrified me. There were plenty of times I wanted to tell that teacher I could not do it, and I was not going to do it without reading it off the paper. Well, not only did I accomplish the goal of memorizing the poem, but I did it with such confidence, I shocked myself.

My point is we would rather run away from something because it looks a certain way instead of really testing it out for ourselves. I may have recited that poem while in middle school, but would you believe that once I decided to go to college, my English professor had us do the same exact thing? I was like, oh man, I know this one, and again without hesitation, I knocked it out the park.

Some, if not majority, of the roads we will have to travel in this lifetime would be those that one day we will travel again. Not too often, we will encounter something again our paths that will never happen again. This is why we must be very careful how we handle this along our journeys. We cannot be so quick to write off people, places, and things. Now, I do believe there are some things we need to leave where they are; some roads we should not travel back down. I am not referring to those things, but simply those that will take us off the road towards purpose.

God has given each one of us a path or a road to travel in life. That road comes with detours, dead ends, four-way stops, bumps, and holes. Our main task is to just keep going. At times it may look dark and scary, like your worst enemy could be standing down there, but your focus is to keep going. I cannot tell you how many times I was faced with a road that looked as if I was the only person ever to travel it. I mean, I wanted to give up again, but I kept going.

The perfect example is when you first decide you will give your life to Christ. You become excited about your new journey. Then one day, your life takes an unexpected shift, tossing things upside down. In that moment, God will send messengers to help guide you. On your journey, God will have different messengers that will be in position to help lead and guide you down those less-traveled roads. Usually, when you feel all alone like no one else is there, is when you will find that person standing. But it takes for you to be in position. Your heart must also be in the right posture to receive. Granted, we are not always open to receiving help. I know for sure that is my biggest issue. But when I receive confirmation from God, I know the road becomes easier to bear.

Life will be hard; you will have those days where it seems like nothing will go right. You just have to be mindful of the little messengers along the way. It could honestly be anything. In order to see and hear, you must be opened to seeing and hearing. Your heart must be available, but your mindset must also be transformed. Understand that not every road will be rough and rigid like a dirt road, but it will lead you to a place designed just for you. In this season, we have to take our birthing seriously. We have to recognize when it is time to leave the cocoon and spread our wings. I have reached that stage, and I see that the world awaits me. I believe I am ready to take flight.

16

Taking Flight

This process has been closely related to that which one would have if they were to give birth. In other cases, the process of a caterpillar becoming the butterfly. Believe it or not, I see myself in both places. I view this very moment as the birthing of something new. I see myself as a butterfly that has discovered her new wings. I am positioned and ready to test out life on exciting levels.

Words cannot explain what I am really feeling in this very moment as I think about stepping outside of my comfort zone to take my first flight. To be clear, this year has taught many of us that it was time to fly, and by any means. I literally took my first airplane flight in May of this year. I can recall getting to the airport, and it was empty. I checked in, went through TSA, and started towards the terminal. It was not until I was at the correct gate that I started to develop anxiety. My heart started beating so fast, and I started to really reconsider. I almost decided not to move forward until I recognized God telling me to jump; it's okay.

This was going to become my moment of living beyond my limitations. It was time for me to see the world outside of what I was accustomed to. Once I was seated on the plane, I did what most first-timers probably would do—I prayed. I thanked God for just granting me the chance to see new things, but to also cover me. Once the plane took off and we were sailing across the sky, I felt myself relax, and that's when I saw my rainbow in the sky. I just knew that was all the confirmation I needed to know that God heard from me.

Stepping out on faith is never an easy task. It will be packed with excitement, anxiety, and sometimes fear. When it is time for you to move forward in your process, it will be like the baby eagle and the momma eagle. The nest will become uncomfortable to the point you would not want to remain. The momma will convince you that it is time to take flight, though you have never used your wings. As that baby eagle, you have to have faith that nothing will hurt you. At this moment, you have to totally trust your process.

It is easy for me to sit here and tell you all about my process and how I have been able to get through it. What I really want to do is encourage you throughout every phase of your process. I do not believe you will read another book such as this, but at least I know

you will get to relate to me in a sense. There is so much more that

will come by just taking a moment to breathe, relax, and enjoy the

flight. This is where your real journey continues.

17

Journey Continues

Making the decision to move forward is what we are encouraged to do every single day. Each day that we get a chance and opportunity to try it again is another day to get things right. Just the ability to move forward in any possible way is one of great courage and ability. Not everyone believes they can move on after facing such traumatic experiences. I just thank God that I have been able to move forward along my journey.

You may ask, what's next? What will be the next big thing I birth? I say this you will have to continue to follow the process to see. It is not always good to let everything out of the bag. But I can assure you that my journey will not stop here. I am super excited to be where I am. There have been many things that tried to rob me of my purpose. But because I am a believer and child of God, I know it was only by his grace that I have been sustained.

Once you submit and allow the transformation to really

manifest itself, you will begin to learn so much more about who you are. After this, you should begin to see your journey in a different view. Things you may have forgotten will be brought back to your remembrance. You will experience feelings that you thought may have died. In those moments, you must allow yourself to just be. Your life is the journey that most will desire, for it will be your testimony that will set them free. Continue moving forward; your journey awaits!

Acknowledgments

Wow! I would like to take the time to thank those that have cheered with me throughout this whole process. From the beginning to the end, you guys have stuck with me. I want to thank those individuals that put up with my tears and anxiety. You just don't know how great it feels to be in this moment. I want to thank my daughters for always seeing the greatness in me. I promise you this one will be our best seller. I love you all with every inch of me. I thank all of you that have supported my journey in any way, whether it was purchasing copies of my book, journal, booking a consultation, or becoming a mentee, I thank you. But above all, I want to thank God for keeping me, stretching me, and causing me to rise above all for the sake of his purpose being fulfilled in me. I thank you, thank you, thank you!

About the Author

Ms. Courtney Johnson was born and raised in Orangeburg, South Carolina. She is the mother of three beautiful daughters. She first discovered her love for writing and art at the very young age of four years old. Since then, she has been expressing herself creatively through painting and freestyle writing/journaling. Ms. Courtney attended school in the Orangeburg Public schools. She attended undergrad at South Carolina State University. She attended graduate school at South University, obtaining a master's degree in clinical mental health counseling. Courtney is also a mentor for youth in her community through her nonprofit, Our Q.U.E.E.N.S Mentoring Group. She just enjoys impacting the lives of many, and soon there will be more!

Coach Courtney became certified as a transformation coach through The Power Hub Institute, under Apostle Joshua Johnson. Ms. Courtney is also a talented artist of *The Royal Pallet* and the author of *A Purposeful Journey: The Process of Enduring While Moving Towards a Meaningful Purpose* the book, and art and meditation reflection journal.

Courtney wears many different hats, but her main focus is the coaching strategy that she put in place. It focuses on transformation in these five areas: mind, body, spirit, purpose, and finances. This strategy is facilitated through a transformation coaching model and a series of holistic coaching approaches.

You can connect with Coach Courtney through this platform, subscribing to her YouTube channel, tune in to her podcast, or following her on social media. Either way, Coach Courtney J. is on the move to help change lives, intentionally and purposefully!

www.ingramcontent.com/pod-product-compliance
Lightning Source LLC
Chambersburg PA
CBHW031225090426
42740CB00007B/713